Phenomenal Women

An Anthology of Selected Poems

The Laura (Riding) Jackson Foundation Press

1914 14th Avenue

Vero Beach FL 32960

Phenomenal Women:

First Edition

Laura (Riding) Jackson Foundation Press
An imprint of The Seizin Press Vero
Website: https://www.LRJF.org

Printed in the United States of America
Paperback book: ISBN 13: 978-1-954488-00-7
eBook: ISBN 13: 978-1-954488-01-4

Cover Image: *Moving the Nest*
Used by Permission of the Artist
Sharon Sexton
Vero Beach Florida

In honor of a
phenomenal woman:
Laura (Riding) Jackson

Acknowledgements

In collaboration with the American Association of University Women (AAUW) – Vero Beach Chapter, the Board of the Laura (Riding) Jackson Foundation (LRJF) solicited poems from Florida's poets on the Treasure Coast and Space Coast on the topic of "Phenomenal Women."

Special thanks to our judges: Sean Sexton - Poet Laureate of Indian River County, Cherie Clark, Susan Lovelace, and Jacque Jacobs.

Financial Support for the prizes and publication of this anthology was provided by:

The Joanne and James Mitchell Foundation

Drellag Press, LLC

The Laura (Riding) Jackson Foundation

Special thanks to Sharon Sexton for her generosity in allowing us to use a photograph of her sculpture *Moving the Nest* for the cover of this anthology.

Thanks to Bill Johnston for his assistance with photographs used in this anthology.

Note: This competition was open to poets on the Treasure Coast and Space Coast of east central Florida. All entries were blind reviewed and finalists selected from all submissions.

Laura (Riding) Jackson Foundation

It is a great pleasure for the Laura (Riding) Jackson Foundation to join with American Association of University Women to celebrate "Phenomenal Women." This contest is especially timely as women continue to struggle to achieve recognition equal to their merit and accomplishment in many areas of society.

Phenomenal women are everywhere. Whether in the realm of domesticity, business, or civil affairs—past and present—women of resilience, grit, and bravery have shown the way to survival in difficult circumstances. Those with talent, perception, and generosity have given insight into the complexities of our world while showing a path forward. Indeed, our Foundation recognizes one phenomenal woman in Laura (Riding) Jackson and her tenacious focus on her search for the truth through her works of poetry, criticism, essays, stories, and finally a "fundamental reevaluation of language itself" in her dictionary, *Rational Meaning*.

It has been a pleasure to read the submissions; each is a tribute, an honor, to a phenomenal woman. The breadth of cultures referenced reflects the reality—in all times and in all places—that there are women whose energy, intelligence, and determination is inspiring the next generation.

Stroking memory to tease out detail, our featured writers enrich our understanding of these "phenomenal women." The reader is drawn into both the "who" and the "why" by the deft use of imagery and poetic form. What an outstanding picture each submission offers! One can't help but think that bringing all these women together would make for an interesting dinner party!

Congratulations to the winners of the Phenomenal Women Poetry Competition! Your submissions inspire us to pause and reflect, and to remember the truth of a phenomenal life.

Thanks to all!

Marie Stiefel
President, Laura (Riding) Jackson Foundation
April 2023

American Association of University Women
Vero Beach Florida

We were promoting a fundraiser called "Phenomenal Women, A Cabaret" by Ami Brabson to raise money for scholarships for young women in Indian River County when one of our members, who is also on the Board of the Laura Riding Jackson Foundation (LRJF), suggested a poetry contest on the same theme. The works chosen from that contest have become this lovely book. How surprised and thrilled we were that LRJF wished to amplify our event, making it more of community project than a fundraiser alone.

During the cabaret, Ami Brabson brought to life nine poets, authors and singers – phenomenal all – some of whom we hadn't known. She highlighted their brilliance (and hers). At the end of her show, we were pleased to have the three highest-placing winners of this contest read their poems about the phenomenal women who had inspired them. The themes and our organizations worked together beautifully.

The two organizations have worked together before. We've known each other and participated in events together. The alliance around this poetry endeavor has advanced our relationship further, and we thank this collaborative organization for reaching out to us and into the community.

We applaud phenomenal women everywhere—and now in these pages–for their beauty, bravery, resilience and inspiration.

Linda Barker

President

American Association of University Women

Vero Beach Branch

April 2023

CONTENTS

FIRST PLACE: Janna Schledorn – Cento for Cheryl Boyce-Taylor . . .   1

SECOND PLACE: Michael Howard – Nora, a Students Lament   3

THIRD PLACE: Roseangelina Batista – Cotton Queen.   7

Roseangelina Batista – Coffee King. 11

Adriana de Kanter – Barbara Jordan:
To be with her was to know greatness. 15

Valerie Gallucci – About Phenomenal Women, Some Known 17

Valerie Gallucci – Heroic Quatrains for a 12-Year Womanhood 19

Valerie Gallucci – Big Sister Figure 23

Jackie Grady – Aunt. 25

Jackie Grady – Iranian Women a Poem for the Protests 27

Michael Howard – Death of a War Correspondent 29

Jeanne Selander Miller – A Long Line of Strong Women 33

Jeanne Selander Miller – Ode to my Foremother 37

Joanne Mitchell – The Day I was Judas 39

Joanne Mitchell – Madness. 41

Diane Morgan – Drowning Time 43

Jennifer Pellegrino – This Is My Mother 45

Fay Picardi – They Also Serve 47

Janna Schledorn – Ode to the Art Teacher 49

Janna Schledorn – Wild 51

Sara Smith – On The Spectrum 53

About the Poets 55

Janna Schledorn

Cento for Cheryl Boyce-Taylor

Dear Audre, Lucille, Adrienne,
I want to be a badass grown woman poet like you
filled with birth stories and moon's sickled lamp,
scraps of poems hidden in cupboards, pen waiting,
pretending not to need.

Like you, piecing wounds into slingshot songs,
girlfriends arranging flowers—
hibiscus, amaryllis, sunflowers, bright bitter marigolds,
crimson orchids, morning glories, lilacs, blue petunias,
peonies, hydrangeas, baby's breath, white tulips, sage—

white sage burning for my lost son,
red mist of words, wild African strawberry bark tea
mournful wailing Florida water
ah write   ah write   dem down
not everybody know to write *dauter*
stay in bed, sleep as late as you want, dream
white tulips, white sage, hydrangeas, hibiscus
misery eh ah color that does look good on me nah

Where does it say we should not question God?
"Who is holding a gun to your head and preventing you
from saying the things you must say?"

like Florida water broke skin meh dauter womb
bless yuh little hand that choose de pen gone searching

Michael Howard

Nora, a Student's Lament

You were rare indeed Nora,
A Miss, I hoped, when you clicked in
On high heels with unusual confidence and class,
Sat on your desk, not behind it.
A short skirt, unique for our teachers,
Showcased muscular legs and strong thighs,
Peeked and tweaked my adolescent interest.
Your auburn hair pulled tight, with a youthful tie
In back while an air of erotic sophistication engulfed
Our class like heavy smoke from a smoldering fire.
Your indifference amped my romantic daydreams.

You pushed your glasses up and back,
Stylish and brazen and
Then you spoke.

Not syrup southern we'd dulled into daily,
Nor prudish and provincial like the others,
But European. German, Austrian perhaps.
A mysterious goddess here to shove

Latin, German, and mythology
Down our lowly throats.

Now, your ancient gods spoke to me.
I befriended Homer, set sail in the Iliad and Odyssey.
Apollo sang to us while I slept with
Edith Hamilton.
Nora, you were my Venus. As Neptunem
I lured you to my lair by the sea.

You opened Europe to us, and the war.
Told us of your lover, a young soldier,
Lost somewhere in the fight and chaos.
He had a special tattoo on his shoulder.
You searched for him. Had he forgotten you?
Then at Leipzig med school you saw
The cadaver with that special tattoo.

Years later I searched for you.
I wanted to show you what I'd become,
The places I'd been, things I'd seen.
You'd had hope for me, saw promise,
Admired my restless spirit, my interests.
You had inspired me.
I needed to tell you.

But your Gods left long ago.

Only Apollo sang quietly in the distance.

You had grown old, lost somewhere, too.

If only you'd had a special tattoo.

Ah, but Nora,

I am still Neptune.

And you are still with me

In my lair by the sea.

Roseangelina Batista

Cotton Queen

for my grandmother Isabel of Lisbon

O Lisbon *queen*!

Give me your cambric cotton,
Lace embroidered from Arroios,
White-shroud for my Azorean father.

O Lisbon *queen*!

Regent of the olive trees!
Give me the cambric cotton
Stitched into handmade rag dolls.

O Lisbon *queen*!

Isabel, the redemptress.
Give me your alabaster story,
Render it black and brown.

Yes, little child, yes!

I tell you, grandpa was a drought migrant,
Timberland chopper, forest arsonist,
Tenant of three crop seasons, hunter.

O Lisbon *queen*!

Tell me the loveliest tale,
Embroidered from Arroios!

Yes, little child, yes!
Arranged marriage of cousins,
Dreaded lightning strikes, knife
Fights, deep wells. Snakes
Hissing on beams, clouds
Of venom, cotton tree bugs,
Endless market payments,
Floggings in the fields,
Stalks of sugar cane.

Tears of children,
Cattle eating clothes
Dying on the grass.
Surge of bees, wild
Cassavas, bitter scarlet
Eggplant, bean pods
Stripped of leaves.

O Lisbon *queen*!

Yes, little child, yes!
Hollowing the earth,
Cleaning the seedlings,
Fashioning their cradles.

May blossom of bolls,
Great harvest, good thing!

Crop huts full and white
As the June moon, laden
Trucks lope along dirty
Red roads, belch plumes
Into cerulean village
Skies
O child of Lisbon!

Roseangelina Batista

Coffee King

When coffee was king, *Grand-mère*
Ernestina das Dores was born in Sao Paulo.
Millions of tons moved from plantation alley
hauled by thousands of pack-mule trains on the
narrow dirt trails to Santos Port.

Old growth forests felled to clear the land trunks
burned naked the stark shift from cane to coffee.
Three seedlings inserted into holes meters apart
Aligned rows shielded by cornstalks.

Hoeing till dusk uprooted weeds, pruned branches
blackened by frost-killing *sauva* ants storming the roots.
Coffee trees blossomed like bridal trains, snow white
in four years, mature at four meters feted
when the *colonos* contract expired.

Ernestina's family tended two thousand grove trees,
dwelled in one of dozen hamlets far from the great house
close to the cemeteries where slaves were buried
without a head stone.

Myriad gangs of men, women and children
speaking Italian Japanese Spanish stripped whole

branches bare ripe withered berries
fell upon the sheets beneath. She gathered
up three hundred liters per day.

The coffee washed in vats of water culled from gutters
and terraces, berries spread out to dry on the stones.
Pulp shells desiccated, cracked, turned three times
on daylight terrace heaped at night, hulled
by wooden tip-hammers or under cattle hooves.

Broken shells blown away in huge rattan sieves
Then, spread on the table, hand-sorted and bagged
at sixty kilograms each. Shipped to the port
where wharf Samsons wield five-bag stacks on bare
shoulders.

The coffee brokers fixed the account books of the great
estate, the *latifundio* for the pureblood Lusitanian heirs.

To the landless brown militia:
Scarecrows, cane brandies, whipping posts.
To the mounted ranch hands: Three mouthfuls of rice.
For the landlord's mulatto children: hoe handles.
The mixed blood children's lives solid as pieces of
sliced pork imbibed in tallow tins.

And so, she married on this *fazenda*, the year
coffee slept as a king and awakened a beggar
after the killing frost. The same year locust

plagues decimated the sharecrops and Spanish flu invaded the plantation. The year of the First War.

Trees survived Death's debris, the fertilizer of new growth crops. But for me she kept only the memory of seeing Halley's Comet twice:

Once in 1910, and again in 1986.

Both at coffee harvesting time.

Adriana de Kanter

Barbara Jordan:
To be with her was to know greatness.

Before Amanda Gorman's mighty roar,
another famous female orator's
voice of God thundered majestic.

Every syllable, clearly modulated, the
cadence like a melodramatic march,
waxing–waning, crescendo—release.

Like an imam's call to prayer
like a preacher's call for redemption
like a negro spiritual calling us home.

Political prophet, eloquent equalizer,
Black Jesus spoke with knowing guile,
truths from her wide, smiling lips.

Her hands acted a kabuki dance drama;
she jabbed the air at verbs with verve,
fingers confirming crucial concepts.

She demanded total attention.
Demanded deepest comprehension.
Demanded common minds understand.

Ebony granite, monumental and thick,
erect in her wheelchair, her
legs withered and thin and sick.

She would not retreat from reason.
Her faith in the Constitution whole,
complete, total. A patriot's pledge.

A black American's sacred promise,
articulating our shared past, our destiny.
We the people. All the people.

Valerie Gallucci

About Phenomenal Women, Some Known

She folds tin foil around three 'bread and butter' sandwiches–the kids call them that. / It feels like tar is hardening around the joints in her fingers. / She has memorized and recited book excerpts to win men's hearts. / She pulls over, plucks a frog from the side of her car, and deposits it in the grass. / Her voice transmits a cutesy news story through the college town's airwaves. / She and her husband work, three months on, one month off, cleaning cruise ship cabins. / Her plane collides with the North Tower. / Cotton dust, visible in the factory air, enters her lungs. / Millions of people watch her makeup tutorials. / She is the first time a black girl sees herself in a character. / This is her second time as someone's Maid of Honor. / People are starting to believe her when she says she doesn't want children. / She can't read street signs or restaurant menus. / Her dream school's logo smiles up at her from the top of an acceptance letter. / She places red peppers onto her gas stove's flames and collects them once they are soft and charred. / When he, red-eyed, says "Never again," she believes him. / She loves herself in a world that has told her to do the opposite. / Her life has been reduced to four walls and a television, but she still exudes light and joy. / She has faced the demons of generational trauma. / There is a dog food cookbook in her kitchen. / She is waiting for a text back. / Her face still has some baby fat. / She is a woman and not a teen and she doesn't feel old yet. / At the grocery store, she scans the plastic gallons of milk for her daughter's birthday. / Tabloids display her cellulite on their front covers. / Her stomach has fallen. / She has known the knees-to-the-floor kind of heartbreak. / She is a therapist who tells her clients, all women, that they will fall in love many times.

Heroic Quatrains for a 12-Year Womanhood

At eighteen my refrain was "I am a
woman but I don't feel like one." I drew
tattoos for an all-woman Shakespeare play.
My phenomenal womanhood was new.

Nineteen and sporting an undercut, I
felt like a good witch gliding downhill on
my bicycle: dress hem fluttering, high
on endorphins, facing a pastel dawn.

Americans don't say "swimming costume"
I told French girls at dinner, age twenty.
Their house was full of fresh food to consume,
and my body, bright and strong, ate plenty.

Before twenty-one, I never tallied
eight lines on paper to witness the day's
dreaded length. In my dreams, women rallied
for work life balance. I missed the sun's rays.

Twenty-two began with my girl, not there–
orange tabby remains, the neighbor's yard.
Gorgeous in grief, I was caught in his stare,
this predator who could smell a downed guard.

Moving to a city twelve hundred miles
north was a privilege. Chicago saved me
from a man. She was all mosaic tiles,
party colored, brightening twenty-three.

At twenty-four, I had long curly hair,
a new boyfriend, and a therapist with
words like "codependent;" I didn't care.
To a younger me, his love was a myth.

I was still in love at twenty-five, but
my insides writhed from the pressure–pleasure
was evasive, my masters caused a rut,
I think. Resentment is hard to measure.

Florida welcomed me back. My cheek had,
like old citrus, been bruised. Florida saw
nothing but a woman who'd left two bad
men by age twenty-six, tired and raw.

Twenty-seven was the year of National
Parks, of opening my eyes to beauty
in the West, and being more rational.
To myself I had the highest duty.

Forgiveness was twenty eight's lesson–to
be kind to the version of me who thought
staying was the best thing I could do,
that, if things ended, my time was for naught.

Now, I am a woman and I feel like one.
I collect clown earrings and cute tattoos.
Womanhood, still phenomenal and fun,
is something I would never want to lose.

Valerie Gallucci

Big Sister Figure

You said for every sign of wear there
was a lesson learned—that your body
reflected your mind like a tree's
branches and its roots.
Did I know that ants farm aphids, ingest
the sweet goo they draw from their
host plant? You showed me a picture of a
stand-off between an ant and a ladybug
who wanted to devour the
former's meal tickets.
You used phrases like "elbow grease"
and "a bee in her bonnet," things that
would make people say they
hadn't heard that in a long time,
much to your delight.
Once, you left a care package at my
apartment door. I still remember your angular
handwriting—like a new font. Another
time, when we were both at the door,
you assessed the window and
advised that I add plants.
I didn't understand until I saw your

place, where you kept succulents in
the street-facing windows. "They get
the best sun here," you explained, "and they obscure
the view from outside."
The back windows, more private, were
landing pads and vantage points for your cats.
Your backyard had well-stocked
feeders and bird baths.
The cats were enraptured by the symphony of
wildlife, chittering and pawing at the glass.
There were small worlds back there:
citrus trees fertilized by a bee colony.
The nectar they collected yielded
orange blossom honey.

Aunt

Rain fell
>   thick and slushy
>   soon to be snow,
she stomped her feet,
her rubber boots yawning as she yanked them over her
ankles
>   and placed them by the door to sit in their puddles.
She would die someday,
>   But not today.
That thought would be pushed until I moistened her lips
with a sponge
>   softening the broken skin, cut from ragged, shallow
breaths.

No instead today she held the box from a bakery
>   its flimsy white lid flipped back.
>   Donuts.
I picked the chocolate filled,
my cousin the powdered.
>   Sometimes I'd eat two.
These are the memories of my Saturday morning sleepovers.

She was my evergreen

>Every event, holiday and birthday

>The first to arrive, the last to leave

>Even during those years when I had no space for
family;

>She'd puncture the silence of my sullen mood with a
"hello!" or "goodbye!"

When I returned to deliver her eulogy

>changing into my black dress before the mirror

>hanging on the wall of my childhood bedroom

I kept waiting and waiting and waiting,

>expecting to hear her voice

>filtering down the hall.

And that absence

>was my first memory

>of her gone.

Jackie Grady

IRANIAN WOMEN
A POEM FOR THE PROTESTS

Her hijab slips,
baring the delicate skin of her neck,
and she is kissed with bullets
instead of by lips.

Michael Howard

Death of a War Correspondent

I find her in the photo lying prone along a trail
Where she has bled and died. I know this, not by the caption,
But by the sheen of what has pooled around her neck.
It is the last photo on the last page of his collection,
A posthumous book tribute to her life's work as a War
Correspondent.
It is the only photo in his collection that she did not take.

A trip wire and mine found her where the slosh of Vietnam
Rice paddies and sharp-edged elephant grass merge.
Her bush hat lies close by, blown clear by the blast.
It was her calling card, like her horn-rimmed glasses and
Pearl earrings from Tehran. They all went home with her.
The photo, like all of hers, is black and white,

Best to tell the stark contrast between life and death,
The fine line she bravely walked for a very long time.
Beside her kneels a Navy Chaplain, there to deliver last
rights.
Marines stand behind, bewildered by yet another death.
She was one of their own and war took its sweet time to kill
her.
His book title reads *Dickey Chapelle Under Fire,*

First American Female War Correspondent
Killed in Action. It is not a book or title she sought.
But she knew well the risks, had always burned glass ceilings,
Pushed and clawed into the brutal, closely guarded realms of men,
Unafraid as sniper rounds buzzed past her like irritant wasps
In the desolate bomb craters of Iwo Jima and Okinawa.

"No place for a woman," the generals had said.
She once befriended Michener on the bridge at Andau
Where they both told the world how the Hungarians
Fled Soviet occupation and brutality.
Arrested by communists, she stood steadfast,
Endured the anguish of interrogation, uncertainty,

And seclusion in the infamous Fo Street Prison.
She feared not the French and secreted her way
Into the Algerian rebel camps to speak for them,
She, a woman among Arabs. She, their voice,
Silenced prior as if the surrounding Sahara and
Atlas Mountains conspired to mute their cause.

She eluded Batista's secret police, worked her way into
Cuba's rugged Sierra Maestra, where she sat beside Castro
And reported on yet another exploding revolution.
Exposed to the harsh realities of life in caves and combat and the

Relentless discomfort offered free by an indifferent jungle,
She wrote and photographed. She reported the raw truth as
she saw it.

Soldiers and Marines mourned her death.
She was one of their own, a love and honor
Bestowed on few save their brothers,
Those damn few who fought and died beside them.
Her biography title reads *Fire in the Wind,* and
She truly was a Fire in the Wind to the very end.

Jeanne Selander Miller

A Long Line of Strong Women

Pondering
Who might I have become
without my mother, my father, and my family?

There is so much more to one's life than is etched upon a
tombstone.
What happened in between and is signified by that simple
hyphen?
August 26, 1853-February 3, 1933

Where were you born?
The vital records disagree, most say Pennsylvania. No city
or county given.
No birth certificate exists.
Baptized in Antrim, Ireland only a few months later?
Doubtful.
Ireland was in the midst of the Great Famine. No one was
returning, not then.

Your parents? Both dead and buried before 1857.
Just a young girl, only four years old, too young to
remember or recount the story
of how or why
you traveled alone on an orphan train to a station in north
central Iowa.

Carrying only your given name,
attached with a safety pin on an old hand-me-down coat.

Did you have any brothers or sisters?
No stories remain.
How many times did you disembark onto a platform in
rural towns all across America?

Did you pray someone kind would take you in?
Were those who came to look you over hoping for a field
hand,
someone strong enough to help with the farming?
Were you overlooked because you were so young?
Were you overlooked because you were a girl?
It hurts my heart to imagine. How did you bear it, so young
and all alone?

Some orphaned children were adopted, others became
indentured servants.
Taken in by Thomas and Mary Daily Mackin.
Never adopted. Never took their name.
The story of life with the Mackins has been lost and may
never be told.
Neither the census of 1860 nor 1870 bears your name.
Unacknowledged? Were they good to you?

An indentured child, bound in service until seventeen,
given in marriage to Francis Duffy.

Nine months from the date of your marriage, Daniel, your
first child, was born.
The first of ten.

Did you learned to be strong, resilient, and how to love
under the tutelage of Mary Daily Mackin?
Was she your alchemist?
Against all odds, did she turn a life fraught with hardship,
danger, and peril
into a life of pure gold?
Or were you always golden, only needing to be buffed to
shine?

Your legacy lives on—
your youngest son, my grandfather,
Leo Joseph Duffy
a good and honest man—kind, loving, and hard-working.

Mary Ann McCloskey
Loved, honored, and remembered.
You earned the titles
Great and Grand
Mother

Jeanne Selander Miller

Ode to my Foremother

Alice Burns
Born in 1812 to Irish Catholic parents
in the townlands of Tullyallen in County Armagh
in the British occupied land now known as Northern Ireland
Tracing your family's presence in the land of Ulster
back to the first century of the common era
descendants of Chieftains and Kings
Entrapped in a life of rampant
poverty and ethnic discrimination
Siblings— too many to count
Names, gender, and vital statistics lost to history
One of many poor, unschooled born in your place in time
Given in marriage when still a girl
to Patrick Duffy
Teenage mother when your first was born
Fifteen children in twenty-some years
Twelve sons and three daughters
All born on Irish soil
Just scraping by, subsisting, and
keeping your children both clothed and fed
Tenant farmers
Working the land

where the rents were dear and
the fruits of your labor were harvested
and handed over to the landowners—
by laws imposed under British dominion
Then the blight took out the potato crop
Famine hit the land and starvation claimed over one million souls
Emigrate or perish
Victims of the Irish diaspora scattered like seed in the wind
Away from our ancestral homeland
A family of seventeen starts over
Homesteading eighty acres of the rich, dark Iowa earth
in the breadbasket called America
Woman
Wife
Mother
Ever faithful, steadfast, loyal, and true
Enumerable sacrifices made in the daily struggle
And thus,
all of your children survived
Well done
Alice Burns

Joanne Mitchell

THE DAY I WAS JUDAS

Mom, the homeroom mother
The planner of parties
For my class
It's Christmas time
And this day was the Christmas party.
Right on time, she walked through the
door With all the goodies for the party
Then I saw her.
What did she do to her hair?
Her neighbor gave her a
permanent Her hair looked like
Frankenstein Short, hard, and full
of tight fuzz Looked like it was
singed.
The kids laughed
Who is she?
I answered
I do not know.
With the burnt hair.
She came through despite knowing how she
looked She came for me
Never stopped being my
mom.

Joanne Mitchell

MADNESS

On the visit to Mary Todd's home
There were several references to her madness. How life
affects one is unpredictable
In one's life, events direct one to the road to madness.
Her mother dies when she is six
She was one of sixteen kids
Many kids' parents have a hard time getting around to all
Four girls and three boys; first family Dad marries a second
time
There are five girls four boys Sixteen in all.
Then several of her brothers die New mom pregnant all the
time How is she ever heard?
How is she ever loved?
How is she ever listened to when she cries? Then she
marries
Has three sons
Husband runs for president He is elected.
Move to Washington Loves pretty clothes;
Ridiculed for how she dresses
Part of her family are Confederate soldiers and
sympathizers of the south Ridiculed again
Civil war ends.
With a great loss to our nation Three of her four sons die

Sons, fathers, uncles, and all those men Of which she must
have taken to her soul.

The fight that divided so many and lost so many

Then he is assassinated while out for a relaxing evening play.

She is kept from her husband's bed as he lays dying

Had to beg for money; a pension if you will Last son puts
her in a mental ward

Too many losses

How is she ever heard? How is she ever loved?

How is she listened to when she cries? Madness in her case

Just called normal.

Diane Morgan

DROWNING TIME

Somewhere
A woman is drowning.
Her hair is alien seaweed
Her lips the color of a sigh
Half caught, half breathed,
Bubbling life against the dark water.

Her eyes are water wide
    and deep,
Wild blue fishes
In a fishless pond.

Her hands are fins,
Delicate and sharp,
Pale as the wind.
Scratching the water.
The water keeps on flowing
Dark and pure.
The wind blows
Empty.

The drowning takes forever,

    Many years.

The pond fades. The wind picks up.

Jennifer Pellegrino

This Is My Mother

This is my mother
at the dinner table before the feast she made,
multiple dishes for a weeknight dinner because she likes
to have a variety.
Her plate is nearly empty,
and she has one elbow on the table,
her head propped up by her hand and her eyes drooping,
the fork slowly making its way up to her mouth as she
forces another bite.
I'm so full, she says.
But now she's forking pushed-aside caramelized onions
and nibbled bits of pastry
and irregular pieces London broil off our plates.
You're not gonna eat that? Wasters! Look, you left the best
part...yum.
And Daddy shakes his head at her but he's trying not to
smile.
My brothers and I make eyes at each other across the table
and our lips twitch
because we're trying not to laugh.
We tell her *Ma, just don't eat anymore.*
But it's so good! she says.

Mommy laughs
and her cheeks are round and strawberry.
She is petite and olive-toned.
Her belly, like Mary Poppins' carpet bag–
small but bottomless.
And now we're all on the linoleum kitchen floor, on our
backs.
Ma's hair is fanned out and we try to lay our heads on her
stomach
so we can feel her laugh
but her voice rings at a pitch when we do,
I'll puke! and then resonates into laughter
and I wish I can laugh like her, with my whole body,
but I put my head on her chest to feel the vibration that
tickles my ear.
And I know that this is my mother.

Fay Picardi

They Also Serve...

(*For Clover Adams*)
Real Change, enduring change, happens one step at a time.
Ruth Bader Ginsberg

Dear Henry,
Haunting, some call this statue,
this *Grief*.
Neither male nor female.
Neither sorrow nor joy.
Inscrutable.
No name, no date, no epitaph.
Among the holly trees, the shrubs of Rock Creek Cemetery,
a surprise, this shrouded figure seated on grey granite.
Draped and cowled, this impassive face reflects the shifting
shadows,
sometimes seems only a shepherd's hood against the rain,
sometimes the frightening faces from our childhood dreams.

Haunting, this bronze statue you commanded for me,
Henry.
You told others I was your original, your unique love, your
model.
And yet, when I resisted your tutelage, your tooling,

you burned my writings, destroyed my paintings, melded
my film.
As a young wife, I wanted to please you.
Others offered me recognition, praise, fame.
From you, I asked only your acceptance.
Yet you continued your mission to mold me.
I struggled to retain that young girl who rode horseback,
who wore a fierce smile framed by untamed curls.
I resisted your attempts at casting me,
my straw bonnet obscuring more and more of my face.

Haunting, this statue, sculpted by your friend, Henry.
Saint Gaudens's finest work, they said.
You declared this masterpiece your final word on the matter.
You never spoke of me again.
But no metal can recast a spirit.
Those who knew me, knew I had no choice.
And those who have come after will search for me,
will question the why and the how.
Standing before this statue,
they will not see a woman, but all women;
looking at this seated figure,
they will not see one man, but all men.
They will search the answers to the why and the how.
And as they find them, they can become
what we could only dream of being, Henry,
our true selves.

Janna Schledorn

Ode to the Art Teacher

One Sunday morning in an elementary school,
temporary church home, the sermon suggests
nothing about us is attractive.
But blue half-faces showcased
on the cafeteria wall invite attention—
cornflower eyes, indigo ears,
navy noses bending to the right
down zig-zag cerulean lines,
vertical rows arranged by grade level,
angled planes of periwinkle
a little lower than the angels—
elementary self-portraits,
beggars and urchins
of whom God is mindful.

The Fourth Grade winks—*our blue*
is not so sad as yours, Picasso,
and we, masters of the fractured profile,
are better than the Third Grade at art.

The teacher must have explained
in a grade-school way,
"Picasso takes a moribund

commemoration of the blandest
kind, and wrenches it back
to thrilling life."

Oh, is this what we look like to you, God?
Flat ceremonial faces
you are breathing into life?

Oh, Picasso!
Thank you for painting us blue.

Oh, Mrs. Heribacka!
Praise for children's art ascending to the ceiling!

Wild

When my parents were falling apart
my big sister kept sending me horses.

Married at nineteen, she moved to Maryland,
must have been near Chincoteague Island.

She sent a palomino mug, brass horse head paperweight,
a wool sweater. Probably the book *Misty*.

I loved the sweater—shimmering moonlight grey,
elegant for an eleven-year-old, outside

soft animal you want next to your skin,
angora, like me more rabbit than horse,

inside the long sleeves, too itchy, too warm
for Florida, too tight for even my skinny arms.

Just touch, unfold from the dresser drawer—

there, right across the chest, a gold, buttery foal
turns and shakes its majestic mane.

My sister, wrapping me
in all those wild ponies.

Sara Smith

On The Spectrum

I smile

Your shoulders tense

I make eye contact

Your eyes connect with the desk

And I know

You are not just another nameless face behind a counter

I see you

I am silent

Passing my slip of paper to you

Making no demand

You breathe easier

How hard is this for you

To look at "us" all day?

Do words cycle through your ears?

Firing up neurons. Combing connections.

Files in the brain snapping open

Searching for synapses to unlock the correct words

until you press down through grinding teeth and force them
from your mouth?

Do you see "our" faces at night in your dreams

Or sleep depleted only to open your eyes to see the light of
another day

And summon the courage you need to show up for work?
You look at me once, nod and write soundlessly
With letters that are rounded and stout
Heavily inked and pressed down dark
Loop and curves are carefully followed and finished
Before another begins
You write on a spectrum, spacing each word so no space is wasted
No crunched letters crushed into the margin
That is something I've never been able to achieve
You are phenomenal
Not marred or marked on the far reaches of a spectrum that notes normal in the middle
When others said you would fail
When others said you should not even try
Did you show them how phenomenal you are?
A woman with courage far beyond what carries me through everyday
A woman with no need to be seen
But I see you
I shine a light on you
You are worth emulating. Celebrating. Applauding.

About the Poets

Rose Angelina Baptista

is a Brazilian-American writer based in Space Coast, Florida. Her recent poems have appeared in or will appear in *Wallace Stevens Journal*, *Joao Roque Literary Journal*, *LitBreak*, and *Gávea-Brown: a Bilingual Journal of Portuguese-American Letters and Studies*.

Adriana deKanter

was a federal civil servant for 36 years (U.S. Senate, U.S. Army V Corp, Office of Governor Ann Richards, U.S. Department of Education, and Asia-Pacific Economic Cooperation). She also was chair of her local Democratic Party. Adriana belongs to poetry-writing groups in Vero Beach and Asheville, where she lives half-time.

Valerie Gallucci

was born and raised in Florida. She lives in Melbourne with her family and loves to romanticize the mundane. She would like to recognize her mom, Sue, sister, Emily, and best friend, Jasmine, as the most phenomenal women she knows!

Jackie Grady

is a Pittsburgh transplant in Vero Beach. She is a lawyer fighting predatory health care billing practices. To escape the daily existential crisis of realizing only healthy people can afford health care, Jackie writes nonfiction and poetry focusing on the themes of the human condition.

Michael Howard

had his first poetry book *The Lightning and the Gale* published in 2022. His second, *Blunt Force Trauma*, is scheduled in 2023. His work has several *Royal Palm Literary Awards in Poetry* by the Florida Writers Association. He is the founding facilitator of the Laura (Riding) Jackson "Pole Barn Poets."

Jeanne Selander Miller

lives in Vero Beach, Florida. She is an award winning author and has written nine books—three are memoir and six are novels. Jeanne dabbles in prose poetry and is a member of the Laura (Riding) Jackson Foundation Tuesday Writers.

Joanne Mitchell

creates poetry as a reflection of her life experience and wisdom and contains humor, angst, pragmatism, spirituality, love and hope that most people don't express. Growing up with eight siblings, experience as a mother, wife, teacher and successful real estate mogul are woven into poetic nuggets of insight for coping with life.

Diane Morgan

is a professional writer. Her latest book, *Secrets of the Manatee: An Insider's Guide to Florida's Most Iconic Marine Mammal* (Pineapple Press), was published in April. Besides manatees, her passions include bloodhounds, Jane Austen, alligators, and gopher tortoises.

Jennifer Pellegrino

is a storyteller, poet, and educator. She writes for children and adults, both in fiction and non-fiction. Jennifer received her Bachelor's in Creative Writing & English and currently works freelance. Born and raised in New Jersey, Jennifer now lives in Vero Beach, Florida.

Fay Picardi

is an internationally published poet who grew up in Kentucky, Mississippi and Virginia. She has studied in France and Italy. She has published three books of poetry; *Nana's Sunday Dance, The Stones Speak,* and *Without Warning: The Marrakech Poems,* as well as a fictionalized biography, *Simonetta,* about Botticelli's muse.

Janna Schledorn

appears in the anthology *Mother Mary Comes to Me, Presence: A Journal of Catholic Poetry, Adanna Literary Journal, Amethyst Review, SWWIM,* and a chapbook, *Those Nine Days.* Co-winner of the 2016 Thomas Burnett Swann Poetry Prize, she teaches at Eastern Florida State College.

Sara Caffrey Smith

has a successful career as a fundraising/marketing professional. She was the Director of Marketing and Communication for Saint Edward's School. She currently writes freelance and her first love is novel writing. Her novel, *Lavender Fields,* was a Dock Street Press Knickerbocker Prize finalist.

The Laura (Riding) Jackson Foundation

The mission of the Laura (Riding) Jackson Foundation is to preserve and interpret the historic home of poet Laura (Riding) Jackson, promote literary programs which nurture passion for the written word, and share the Florida friendly garden surrounding Laura's home. For thirty years the Board has worked to preserve the 1910 homestead of Laura (Riding) Jackson both as an example of environmentally sensitive Florida architecture and as a valued emblem of her significant contributions made in a life devoted to language and literature. The house is located at 6555 College Lane on the Mueller Campus of Indian River State College in Vero Beach. The house is surrounded by a Florida friendly plant garden in honor of the commitment Laura and Schuyler Jackson had to organic farming of the citrus they grew.

With the help of generous partners and supporters, the Foundation sponsors public programs which focus on literature, history, and the relationship of people and the environment. Programs include Teen Writers Workshops, an annual Poetry & Barbecue, Poetry Open Mic, an Oral History Program, Adult Writing Workshops, Bookfairs, and Retreats. We conduct writing groups across genres for adults and offer summer creative writing camps for middle school students.

We have a series of guest speakers at the garden in conjunction with our regularly scheduled open house tours of Laura's historic home. Visit our website https://www.LRJF.org for more information.

Laura (Riding) Jackson Board of Directors (2022-2023)

Officers

Marie C. Stiefel, President

Jacqueline E. Jacobs, PhD, Vice-President for Operations

Susan Lovelace, Vice-President for Programs

Rene Van de Voorde, Secretary

Susan Boyd, Treasurer

Members

Carrie Adams

Cynthia Callander

Cherie Clark

Bruce Fraser, PhD

Andrew Galuska

Jackie Grady

Bonnie McDougall, PhD

Susan McDaniel

Joanne Mitchell

Sean Sexton

Charlotte Terry

Laura (Riding) Jackson Advisory Board (2022-2023)

Laurel Blossom — Poet

Janice Broda — FL Native Plant Society

Elizabeth Friedmann – Authorized Biographer of Laura (Riding) Jackson

Deming Holleran — Poet

Mark Jacobs - Scholar on Laura (Riding) Jackson

Johanna Jones — Former LRJF Board Member

Elliott Jones - Former LRJF Board member

Martha LeMasters — Author, Film Producer

Evelyn Mayerson — Author, Retired University of Miami Professor, Vero Beach Magazine Columnist

Beth Moulton — Former LRJF Board Member, VB Magazine Publisher

Pam Proctor — LRJF Teen Writers Workshop Founder, Author

Chris Ryall — Former LRJF Board Member

Ruth Stanbridge — Indian River County Historian